HARMLESS

Part I
Trilogy: '04-'05-'06

Brett Neveu

BROADWAY PLAY PUBLISHING INC
New York
www.broadwayplaypublishing.com
info@broadwayplaypublishing.com

HARMLESS
© Copyright 2016 by Brett Neveu

Cover art by Rich Sparks

First printing: July 2016
I S B N: 978-0-88145-642-4

Book design: Marie Donovan
Word processing: Microsoft Word
Typographic controls: Adobe InDesign
Typeface: Palatino
Printed and bound in the U S A

HARMLESS was first produced by TimeLine Theatre
Company (P J Powers, Artistic Director) in Chicago,
running from 20 January–18 March 2007. The cast and
creative contributors were:

LIEUTENANT MINDY ERGENBRIGHT.................. Juliet Hart
PRESIDENT DANIEL WESSON ....John Jenkins
JIM MCFEHREN ....David Parkes

Director..Edward Sobel
Scenic designer.. Keith Pitts
Costume designer...Lindsey Pate
Lighting designer ....Charles Cooper
Sound designer.. Josh Horvath
Properties designer.......................................Julia Eberhardt
Dramaturg ....Gabriel Greene
Assistant director... Daria Grubb
Production manager ....Jennifer Martin
Stage manager..Seth Vermilyea

CHARACTERS & SETTING

PRESIDENT DANIEL WILSON, *male, early sixties, President of Prahl College*

JIM MCFEHREN, *male, late-thirties to early forties, Adjunct Professor at Prahl College*

LIEUTENANT MINDY ERGENBRIGHT, *female, mid-thirties to early forties, United States Army Lieutenant*

Time: Spring, 2004
ACT ONE—*a Friday*
ACT TWO—*a Tuesday*

Place: PRESIDENT DANIEL WESSON's *office on the small campus of Prahl College*

ACT ONE

(Lights up on recently renovated older office on the campus of Prahl College, a small liberal arts school in the American Midwest. Within the office are a few books in a bookcase, scattered mementos and a newer heavy desk. On the desk is a computer, a telephone, a few files, a desk lamp and a large blotter. A few newer office chairs sit near the desk and a large desk chair sits behind. Ten or so feet from the desk is a small couch. In front of the couch is a round coffee table and beside the couch is an end table. On the table is a table lamp. A large-ish painting of Ronald Prahl [founder of Prahl College] hangs above the small couch. The door to the office is closed. Sitting on the small couch is JIM MCFEHREN, *an adjunct professor at the school. He wears a button-up shirt, khaki pants and a sport coat. He waits.)*

(An older man and President of Prahl College, PRESIDENT DANIEL WESSON, *opens the office door and enters the office. He wears a shirt, jacket, tie and slacks.)*

PRESIDENT WESSON: Mister McFehren. I'm sorry I'm late.

*(*JIM *stands.)*

JIM: Hello, President Wesson, no no, you're not late.

*(*PRESIDENT WESSON *closes his office door.)*

PRESIDENT WESSON: You've waited.

JIM: It's all right, your assistant told me—

PRESIDENT WESSON: *(Points to outer office)* Jean?

JIM: Yes.

PRESIDENT WESSON: You shouldn't have had to wait—

JIM: Actually, I just got here, I just sat down.

PRESIDENT WESSON: To let you know, the reason you've waited, I was attempting to deal with some traffic cones that were placed in front of the building, some dirty traffic cones, three or four traffic cones lining the sidewalk. I asked Jean to call campus maintenance weeks ago to find out what work was being done, what the purpose was for the traffic cones, and campus maintenance, as usual, gave her the run-around. So there the traffic cones sit, becoming covered with more and more muck and more and more dirt as I walk by them and walk by them day after day. The traffic cones block nothing, they serve no purpose. Today, just now, I felt like moving them, picking them up and moving them, tossing them onto the lawn, that is how fed up I am about those disgusting, useless and intensely annoying traffic cones.

JIM: You should have moved them.

PRESIDENT WESSON: I may yet.

JIM: They are a pedestrian hazard.

PRESIDENT WESSON: Oh my lord, yes. They are. (Pause) Yes. (Beat) Thanks for talking with me today, thanks for taking time to stop by.

JIM: It's no trouble.

PRESIDENT WESSON: It's been awhile since we've spoken face to face.

JIM: Yes.

PRESIDENT WESSON: The last time was a holiday party of some sort last year.

JIM: Right.

PRESIDENT WESSON: We chatted, but only for a few minutes. I hear you've got another one in.

JIM: I do.

PRESIDENT WESSON: That's wonderful.

JIM: Thank you.

PRESIDENT WESSON: Terry Bovenkamp sends me word every time one of our faculty is published.

JIM: She does?

PRESIDENT WESSON: Yes.

JIM: I'll have to thank her.

PRESIDENT WESSON: *The McLine Journal*?

JIM: Yes.

PRESIDENT WESSON: Where can I get myself a copy of *The McLine Journal*?

JIM: I can make a photocopy of my copy, if you'd like.

PRESIDENT WESSON: I can buy a copy.

JIM: I can photocopy my copy for you.

PRESIDENT WESSON: What's the title?

JIM: *Bicentennial Saucer.* It's about a sledding accident.

PRESIDENT WESSON: Fiction?

JIM: Yes.

PRESIDENT WESSON: Plenty of fiction for it not to be considered non-fiction but enough non-fiction to make it interesting fiction?

JIM: The story is loosely based on an incident from my childhood, an incident in which a wooden sled was mildly fractured.

PRESIDENT WESSON: How have you fictionalized the incident?

JIM: The fracturing of the sled has a more tragic result.

PRESIDENT WESSON: I'd very much like to read *Bicentennial Saucer.*

JIM: I would like that.

(A pause)

PRESIDENT WESSON: How are you holding up?

IM: I'm fine.

PRESIDENT WESSON: I've heard some faculty are concerned.

JIM: Not really.

PRESIDENT WESSON: Everyone is speaking some, I suppose, students and faculty.

JIM: Yes.

PRESIDENT WESSON: Which faculty?

JIM: People aren't really speaking that much.

PRESIDENT WESSON: Are your students speaking?

JIM: Some.

PRESIDENT WESSON: Information around here moves pretty fast.

JIM: Yes.

PRESIDENT WESSON: It's like a big family. One big family. Everyone listening, spreading thoughts quickly until everything comes back around.

JIM: Yes.

PRESIDENT WESSON: Like a big family.

JIM: I hadn't spoken to any of my students directly about anything that would cause anyone to worry.

PRESIDENT WESSON: You have spoken to your students?

JIM: Yes. But not much.

PRESIDENT WESSON: You should limit your discussion.

JIM: I've only answered a few questions.

PRESIDENT WESSON: But set limitations.

JIM: I have.

PRESIDENT WESSON: Has he tried to contact you at home?

JIM: No.

PRESIDENT WESSON: Please let me know if he tries to contact you at home.

JIM: I don't think he'll do that.

PRESIDENT WESSON: I've spoken to his parents.

JIM: You have?

PRESIDENT WESSON: You've had some time to speak with Professor Bovenkamp?

JIM: Yes, a few days ago.

PRESIDENT WESSON: She gave you some advice?

JIM: She suggested a few tactics.

PRESIDENT WESSON: What were her suggestions?

JIM: She suggested he should have lessened the detail to enhance the emotional weight. She suggested he read a short story titled *Man's Tooth* by Steven Starley.

PRESIDENT WESSON: *Man's Tooth*?

JIM: Yes.

PRESIDENT WESSON: By Steven Starley?

(PRESIDENT WESSON *writes the title and author on an odd scrap of paper.*)

JIM: Yes.

PRESIDENT WESSON: You had him read the suggested story?

JIM: I suggested he read it.

PRESIDENT WESSON: When does *Man's Tooth* take place?

JIM: The early nineteen-seventies. In Vietnam.

PRESIDENT WESSON: What is *Man's Tooth* about?

JIM: I actually haven't finished it yet. *(Beat)* What I believe Professor Bovenkamp wanted him to understand is how the writer may view characters which have unique internal struggles.

PRESIDENT WESSON: You still recommended the story even though you yourself hadn't finished it?

JIM: Professor Bovenkamp recommended it, so I didn't see a problem.

PRESIDENT WESSON: This isn't related to your current issue of neglecting to read stories others have given to you, is it?

JIM: No, it's not.

PRESIDENT WESSON: Read the story.

JIM: I will.

(A pause)

PRESIDENT WESSON: Someone else may be coming in shortly.

JIM: Someone else?

PRESIDENT WESSON: When had you spoken to your writing students?

JIM: I saw a few of them today at Jennings Hall.

PRESIDENT WESSON: Jennings Hall. Built in 1926. Durwood Jennings. A botanist. Jennings Hall was opened during my grandfather's tenure. The lower level floods during heavy rains. The building is at the bottom of a slight hill, that's why it floods.

JIM: I've seen it do that.

PRESIDENT WESSON: You have?

JIM: But I'm glad, though, that the Mayflies are gone.

PRESIDENT WESSON: Oh my, so am I.

JIM: In Van Blair, those things can cover the windows.

PRESIDENT WESSON: There's nothing like looking out the window to hundreds of skinny Mayflies.

JIM: I remember staying late one evening and watching Mayflies drip from the street lights.

PRESIDENT WESSON: We've gotten them so bad we've had to call out the bulldozers. It gets to be like an oil slick on the roads. You see piles of Mayflies along the embankment.

JIM: I had twenty of them in my shower last year.

PRESIDENT WESSON: Twenty?

JIM: I opened the shower curtain and one, two, three all the way to twenty. I tried to get them all but they're tough.

PRESIDENT WESSON: You mean quick?

JIM: Yes.

PRESIDENT WESSON: Sometimes they're quick and sometimes they're slow. It depends on when you're doing the killing.

JIM: Right.

PRESIDENT WESSON: Mayflies only live a short while.

JIM: I've also had a problem with Japanese beetles.

PRESIDENT WESSON: The orange bugs that pinch?

JIM: Yes.

PRESIDENT WESSON: The bugs that pretend they are ladybugs?

JIM: Exactly.

PRESIDENT WESSON: I have those in my basement. They die in the curtains. In the winter I find their dead carcases scattered on the rug.

JIM: Those bugs also smell.

PRESIDENT WESSON: Like stink-bugs.

JIM: Very much like stink-bugs.

PRESIDENT WESSON: Like boxelder bugs.

JIM: Yes.

PRESIDENT WESSON: Boxelder bugs are a primary nuisance in the summertime.

(A long pause)

(A knock on the office door)

PRESIDENT WESSON: Hello?

(The door opens. Lieutenant Mindy Ergenbright pokes her head into the office. She wears a United States Army uniform.)

LIEUTENANT ERGENBRIGHT: President Wesson?

PRESIDENT WESSON: Hello, yes, hi—

LIEUTENANT ERGENBRIGHT: Your assistant told me to come in—

PRESIDENT WESSON: Hello, come in—

(LIEUTENANT ERGENBRIGHT *enters the office)*

LIEUTENANT ERGENBRIGHT: Hello—

(PRESIDENT WESSON *stands and extends his hand.* LIEUTENANT ERGENBRIGHT *crosses to shake it.)*

PRESIDENT WESSON: It's nice to meet you.

LIEUTENANT ERGENBRIGHT: I'm Lieutenant Ergenbright.

PRESIDENT WESSON: Hello, I'm President Wesson—

LIEUTENANT ERGENBRIGHT: — hello—

PRESIDENT WESSON: — and this is Jim McFehren, one of our Adjunct Professors in fiction writing and Mister Navarro's professor.

LIEUTENANT ERGENBRIGHT: Professor McFehren.

(LIEUTENANT ERGENBRIGHT extends her hand to JIM. He shakes it, but remains sitting.)

LIEUTENANT ERGENBRIGHT: *(To PRESIDENT WESSON)* I just wanted to stop in and say a quick hello.

PRESIDENT WESSON: Hello, Lieutenant Ergenbright!

LIEUTENANT ERGENBRIGHT: Please call me Mindy.

PRESIDENT WESSON: Mindy?

LIEUTENANT ERGENBRIGHT: Yes.

PRESIDENT WESSON: What if I decided to call you Lieutenant Mindy? *(Laughs)*

LIEUTENANT ERGENBRIGHT: *(Laughs)* No, no, please, just Mindy is fine.

PRESIDENT WESSON: Lieutenant "Just Mindy Is Fine", then? *(Laughs)* Mindy. And you can call Mister McFehren "Jim" if you'd like. And please call me "Daniel". Jim, you may also call me Daniel. So. Mindy, Jim and Daniel. Mindy. Would you like to sit down?

LIEUTENANT ERGENBRIGHT: I only came in to say hello.

PRESIDENT WESSON: Please sit, I insist.

(A beat. LIEUTENANT ERGENBRIGHT sits.)

PRESIDENT WESSON: *(To JIM)* Mindy is with Veterans Affairs.

LIEUTENANT ERGENBRIGHT: I'm not actually with the V A.

PRESIDENT WESSON: You're not?

LIEUTENANT ERGENBRIGHT: The V A is a little shorthanded. I'm with the regular army.

PRESIDENT WESSON: Ah. *(Beat)* Are you staying overnight?

LIEUTENANT ERGENBRIGHT: Yes.

PRESIDENT WESSON: Have you checked into a hotel?

LIEUTENANT ERGENBRIGHT: Yes.

PRESIDENT WESSON: Which hotel?

LIEUTENANT ERGENBRIGHT: The Highlander.

PRESIDENT WESSON: That's one of our nicer hotels on the interstate.

LIEUTENANT ERGENBRIGHT: Good.

PRESIDENT WESSON: It was built in the early 1980s. During sporting events, it fills up rather quickly. Alumni enjoy staying at the Highlander.

LIEUTENANT ERGENBRIGHT: "Highlander" is a Scottish term.

PRESIDENT WESSON: Gaelic, referring to a person from the mountainous part of Scotland north of Glasgow.

LIEUTENANT ERGENBRIGHT: Is the hotel owned by someone from Scotland?

PRESIDENT WESSON: No. *(Pause)* Are you stationed nearby?

LIEUTENANT ERGENBRIGHT: I'm stationed in Georgia. Fort Gillem.

PRESIDENT WESSON: I'd told Jim that you might be stopping by.

JIM: You didn't say someone from the army might be stopping by.

PRESIDENT WESSON: I didn't know it would be someone from the army.

LIEUTENANT ERGENBRIGHT: As I said, Veteran's Affairs is short handed.

PRESIDENT WESSON: *(To* LIEUTENANT ERGENBRIGHT*)*
What do you think of our campus? Ignoring those
traffic cones in the front, what do you think?

LIEUTENANT ERGENBRIGHT: It's nice.

PRESIDENT WESSON: The founder was my grandfather,
Ronald Prahl. He was what one might call an
"intellectual entrepreneur." Personally, I've been here
now for, let's see, fourteen years. Yes. Wow. Fourteen
years.

LIEUTENANT ERGENBRIGHT: That's a long time.

PRESIDENT WESSON: Not nearly as long as some of our
faculty. We have a professor of history that's been with
us for nearly forty years. He refuses to retire and the
students love him. His classes are always some of the
first to be filled. He's an incredible orator. *(Beat)* Where
did you go to school?

LIEUTENANT ERGENBRIGHT: Dalver University. And also
Tallburn.

PRESIDENT WESSON: Dalver is very nice.

LIEUTENANT ERGENBRIGHT: It's big.

PRESIDENT WESSON: I've visited there twice. It's quite
lovely during the fall.

LIEUTENANT ERGENBRIGHT: Parts of it are, yes.

PRESIDENT WESSON: I remember a large grove of thin
trees near campus.

LIEUTENANT ERGENBRIGHT: A grove of trees?

PRESIDENT WESSON: Yes.

LIEUTENANT ERGENBRIGHT: I'm not sure where that
would have been.

PRESIDENT WESSON: Near a large statue.

LIEUTENANT ERGENBRIGHT: I don't recall.

PRESIDENT WESSON: Dalver is also near a rather historical site, isn't it?

LIEUTENANT ERGENBRIGHT: Yes.

JIM: *(To* LIEUTENANT ERGENBRIGHT*)* You're here for Ben?

LIEUTENANT ERGENBRIGHT: I am.

JIM: You've read his story?

LIEUTENANT ERGENBRIGHT: Yes.

JIM: When were you given his story?

LIEUTENANT ERGENBRIGHT: It was faxed to me.

JIM: By whom?

LIEUTENANT ERGENBRIGHT: The staff at the V A.

JIM: *(To* PRESIDENT WESSON*)* Who faxed the story to the V A?

PRESIDENT WESSON: Ryan Guffy.

JIM: Ryan Guffy? When did he get the story?

PRESIDENT WESSON: Monday.

JIM: Why does campus security need the story?

PRESIDENT WESSON: It's just Ryan Guffy.

JIM: Who told him to fax it?

PRESIDENT WESSON: I said it was up to him, Mister McFehren. I'm sorry, I just called you Mister McFehren. We've decided it's Jim, right? It's Jim. *(Pause)* You know, both of you, my wife is actually the only person in this world who calls me "Daniel", so it's a bit off-putting if you address me as "Daniel". I know it was my suggestion, but, if its all right, if both of you, instead of calling me "Daniel", could you call me "President Wesson"? I would appreciate it very much.

JIM: Lieutenant Ergenbright?

LIEUTENANT ERGENBRIGHT: Please call me Mindy.

JIM: What do you do for the army?

LIEUTENANT ERGENBRIGHT: I'm a psychologist.

JIM: For which department?

LIEUTENANT ERGENBRIGHT: The Army's Criminal Investigation Division.

JIM: You're a *criminal* psychologist?

LIEUTENANT ERGENBRIGHT: I'm here currently only as a representative of the V A. Not as a criminal psychologist.

JIM: Okay.

LIEUTENANT ERGENBRIGHT: I'll only be on campus a brief amount of time.

JIM: Is this an emergency situation?

LIEUTENANT ERGENBRIGHT: No.

JIM: Do you think he's going to hurt someone?

LIEUTENANT ERGENBRIGHT: It is typical procedure for the V.A. to recommend—

JIM: A criminal psychologist?

LIEUTENANT ERGENBRIGHT: A *psychologist.*

JIM: For?

LIEUTENANT ERGENBRIGHT: A check-in only.

JIM: Okay.

LIEUTENANT ERGENBRIGHT: I'll try not to be in your hair.

PRESIDENT WESSON: You're not "in our hair."

(A pause)

LIEUTENANT ERGENBRIGHT: Since I'm here, do either of you mind if I take a few moments to ask you both a few brief questions?

PRESIDENT WESSON: No.

(LIEUTENANT ERGENBRIGHT *opens a pocket in her satchel and removes a gold pen.*)

PRESIDENT WESSON: That's a nice pen.

LIEUTENANT ERGENBRIGHT: Thank you.

PRESIDENT WESSON: That is a very nice gold pen. May I see it?

LIEUTENANT ERGENBRIGHT: Yes.

(LIEUTENANT ERGENBRIGHT *hands her pen to* PRESIDENT WESSON.)

PRESIDENT WESSON: It's very nice.

(LIEUTENANT ERGENBRIGHT *digs through her satchel for a note pad.* PRESIDENT WESSON *removes a pen from a desk drawer. It appears similar to her pen.*)

PRESIDENT WESSON: This is mine. I've had it for years. It was a gift I received upon my tenth year as president of Prahl. I've replaced the ink cartridge probably a hundred times. I use it very often. I'm surprised I've never lost it. I keep it inside my desk. *(Pause)* Your pen is very nice, also. Thank you for letting me look at it.

(PRESIDENT WESSON *returns* LIEUTENANT ERGENBRIGHT *her pen as she finds her note pad and places her satchel on the floor.*)

PRESIDENT WESSON: *(To* JIM*)* Would you like to see my pen?

JIM: Yes.

(PRESIDENT WESSON *hands* JIM *his pen.*)

PRESIDENT WESSON: It was a present to myself for ten long and much loved years at this desk.

JIM: It's a very nice pen.

(JIM *scribbles with the pen on a loose piece of paper on* PRESIDENT WESSON's *desk.*)

PRESIDENT WESSON: It's all right if you write on that.

JIM: Thank you.

PRESIDENT WESSON: It's a good pen, isn't it?

JIM: Yes.

PRESIDENT WESSON: Here you go.

(PRESIDENT WESSON *holds out his hand.* JIM *returns the pen to him.*)

LIEUTENANT ERGENBRIGHT: This will be quick.

PRESIDENT WESSON: Fire away.

LIEUTENANT ERGENBRIGHT: It would be nice to get just a few impressions.

PRESIDENT WESSON: Of course.

LIEUTENANT ERGENBRIGHT: Nothing too specific.

PRESIDENT WESSON: Sure.

LIEUTENANT ERGENBRIGHT: *(To* JIM*)* How was Mister Navarro in class?

JIM: How was he?

PRESIDENT WESSON: How did he behave?

LIEUTENANT ERGENBRIGHT: How were his involvement and attitude?

JIM: His involvement and attitude?

(A pause)

PRESIDENT WESSON: Jim?

JIM: Both were fine.

LIEUTENANT ERGENBRIGHT: He participated?

JIM: Yes.

LIEUTENANT ERGENBRIGHT: Was he at all withdrawn?

JIM: No.

LIEUTENANT ERGENBRIGHT: Even occasionally?

JIM: No, but if he was, then only slightly.

LIEUTENANT ERGENBRIGHT: No complaints of lack of sleep, feeling depressed, talk of drinking, going to bars?

JIM: No.

LIEUTENANT ERGENBRIGHT: How are his academics?

JIM: Average.

LIEUTENANT ERGENBRIGHT: His grades are average?

JIM: His grades are actually a bit above average.

LIEUTENANT ERGENBRIGHT: B's?

JIM: Mostly, yes.

PRESIDENT WESSON: *(To* LIEUTENANT ERGENBRIGHT*)* I'll get you a copy of his current academic report.

LIEUTENANT ERGENBRIGHT: Do you have anything else he's written besides *An Unpracticed Correction* that I could take a look at?

JIM: I suppose, yes.

LIEUTENANT ERGENBRIGHT: Anything similar to *An Unpracticed Correction?*

JIM: No.

LIEUTENANT ERGENBRIGHT: Nothing as extreme?

JIM: The story's not necessarily extreme. *Gratuitous,* perhaps, but not extreme.

LIEUTENANT ERGENBRIGHT: Nothing as *gratuitous,* then.

JIM: No. Nothing as gratuitous.

PRESIDENT WESSON: I'll have my assistant get copies of his other writing to you.

JIM: You'll find nothing that reveals what you're looking for.

LIEUTENANT ERGENBRIGHT: I'm not looking for anything.

PRESIDENT WESSON: Jim. Relax.

JIM: Relax?

PRESIDENT WESSON: Adjust your tone.

JIM: My tone?

PRESIDENT WESSON: Bring it down a little.

JIM: Bring it down?

(A pause)

PRESIDENT WESSON: Just to let both of you know, I have a few things I need to tend to in less than an hour.

LIEUTENANT ERGENBRIGHT: I'm sorry—

PRESIDENT WESSON: You'd probably like to go meet with him.

LIEUTENANT ERGENBRIGHT: I would.

PRESIDENT WESSON: Soon, preferably.

LIEUTENANT ERGENBRIGHT: Yes.

PRESIDENT WESSON: Maybe then try sticking to questions that require facts instead of opinions.

(A beat)

LIEUTENANT ERGENBRIGHT: *(To JIM)* May I ask you more about Mister Navarro's actions in class?

JIM: That will require my opinion.

PRESIDENT WESSON: *(To LIEUTENANT ERGENBRIGHT)* Provost Overton has spoken to a few of Jim's students and she has taken a few notes of those discussions, if you'd like to see those notes. Or if you'd like to speak to Provost Overton today, I can dial her up. In fact, if you'd like, she can join us right now. I could dial her up and she could come down here and join us.

LIEUTENANT ERGENBRIGHT: That's not necessary.

PRESIDENT WESSON: For a fresh pair of ears.

LIEUTENANT ERGENBRIGHT: It's not needed.

PRESIDENT WESSON: She could be here in a minute.

LIEUTENANT ERGENBRIGHT: President Wesson?

PRESIDENT WESSON: Yes?

LIEUTENANT ERGENBRIGHT: I want to move ahead.

PRESIDENT WESSON: Obviously.

LIEUTENANT ERGENBRIGHT: Then I can go.

PRESIDENT WESSON: Right.

LIEUTENANT ERGENBRIGHT: I don't require Provost Overton's presence right now.

PRESIDENT WESSON: There's no need to be tentative.

LIEUTENANT ERGENBRIGHT: I'm not being tentative—

PRESIDENT WESSON: Let's move forward.

(A beat.)

LIEUTENANT ERGENBRIGHT: Jim?

JIM: Yes?

LIEUTENANT ERGENBRIGHT: What was the assignment that Mister Navarro was given which produced *An Unpracticed Correction*?

JIM: It was an out of class writing exercise.

LIEUTENANT ERGENBRIGHT: What were the parameters?

JIM: Five to ten pages.

LIEUTENANT ERGENBRIGHT: No, I'm sorry, I guess I'm asking if there was any specific direction he was to take regarding subject matter?

JIM: No.

LIEUTENANT ERGENBRIGHT: He was free to write whatever he'd like?

JIM: Yes.

LIEUTENANT ERGENBRIGHT: Did he have to discuss ideas of topics with you beforehand?

JIM: We had discussed how to choose topics of interest earlier in the semester, so all the students knew what was expected.

LIEUTENANT ERGENBRIGHT: What *was* expected?

JIM: Something interesting. Something unique.

LIEUTENANT ERGENBRIGHT: Something personal?

JIM: Something that would be a challenge.

LIEUTENANT ERGENBRIGHT: A challenge how?

JIM: I wanted them to challenge their preconceived ideas of what fiction writing could be. I didn't wish my students to write basic run-of-the-mill hokum characteristic of the common stack.

LIEUTENANT ERGENBRIGHT: Explain.

JIM: I'm sorry. The tone of this conversation is becoming a bit interrogatory.

(A pause)

LIEUTENANT ERGENBRIGHT: Did… *(Beat)* I'm sorry. *(Pause)* Did you happen to give your students examples of the sorts of stories you considered weren't, "basic run-of-the-mill hokum characteristic of the common stack?"

JIM: Of course.

LIEUTENANT ERGENBRIGHT: That's good. That's a good idea.

JIM: That's what I did.

LIEUTENANT ERGENBRIGHT: It makes the class more interesting for you and for them.

JIM: It does.

LIEUTENANT ERGENBRIGHT: It helps them see parallels in their own work and within published work, too.

JIM: Right.

LIEUTENANT ERGENBRIGHT: What were the story examples you gave to your class?

JIM: The students were assigned the stories *Otto's Coach* by Helen Yeer and *The Petrified Creatures* by Louis Barrows.

PRESIDENT WESSON: Mister McFehren also just told me that it was recommended to him that Mr. Navarro also read *(Looks at note) Man's Tooth* by Steven Starley, a story about Vietnam.

LIEUTENANT ERGENBRIGHT: *Man's Tooth*?

PRESIDENT WESSON: By Steven Starley.

LIEUTENANT ERGENBRIGHT: *(To JIM)* What do both of your examples, *Otto's Coach* and *The Petrified Creatures*—what's the subject matter?

JIM: What are the plots?

LIEUTENANT ERGENBRIGHT: Yes. The plots.

JIM: *The Petrified Creatures* is about two children who are terrorized by an older neighbor who eventually sets fire to the house where the children live. *Otto's Coach* is a semi-basic story about a high school football coach who wishes to perfect his duck-drawing skills before his failing health lays him low.

LIEUTENANT ERGENBRIGHT: Why did you choose those two stories?

JIM: They are good illustrations of non-traditional fiction writing yet both contain commonly dissected plot themes.

LIEUTENANT ERGENBRIGHT: A house fire is a commonly dissected plot theme?

JIM: So is a story about a football coach.

LIEUTENANT ERGENBRIGHT: When I was a child, I remember seeing a house fire in my neighborhood. The house two houses down from mine caught fire on Christmas Eve. The young boy that lived there, who was my same age, he was killed in the fire. The boy burned to death in his bunk bed.

JIM: I'm sorry.

LIEUTENANT ERGENBRIGHT: But that proves your point. My memory of that incident is very clear.

PRESIDENT WESSON: A story of Mister McFehren's — *Bicentennial Saucer*—was recently published in a literary journal.

LIEUTENANT ERGENBRIGHT: Congratulations.

JIM: Thank you.

PRESIDENT WESSON: The story is about a deadly sledding accident involving children.

LIEUTENANT ERGENBRIGHT: It is?

JIM: One sled collides with another sled.

LIEUTENANT ERGENBRIGHT: Killing a child?

JIM: One of the sleds is wooden and one of the sleds is metal.

LIEUTENANT ERGENBRIGHT: The wooden sled fractures?

JIM: Yes.

LIEUTENANT ERGENBRIGHT: A piece of the wooden sled stabs another child?

JIM: One of the wooden sled's metal runners becomes detached and cuts across the neck of another child.

LIEUTENANT ERGENBRIGHT: Causing suffocation?

JIM: Breaking his neck.

LIEUTENANT ERGENBRIGHT: That must have been a steep hill.

JIM: The hill was very steep but quite short and icy.

LIEUTENANT ERGENBRIGHT: Giving the sled the speed to injure.

JIM: Those wooden sleds also weigh quite a bit.

LIEUTENANT ERGENBRIGHT: The metal sled is a metal saucer sled?

JIM: These days most of them are plastic.

LIEUTENANT ERGENBRIGHT: I had a metal saucer sled. It was a big yellow smiley face.

JIM: Mine was a roundish American Flag.

LIEUTENANT ERGENBRIGHT: A "Bicentennial Saucer?"

JIM: Right.

LIEUTENANT ERGENBRIGHT: Does the story take place after the sled accident?

JIM: It does. The father, he had purchased the saucer sled for his son, the father is plagued by the death of the boy his son accidently killed.

LIEUTENANT ERGENBRIGHT: How does the father handle it?

JIM: He sits on a park bench. It's wintertime, so he sits on a snowy park bench.

LIEUTENANT ERGENBRIGHT: I'd like to read *Bicentennial Saucer* sometime. It sounds interesting.

JIM: I'll print one off for you.

LIEUTENANT ERGENBRIGHT: Thank you.

PRESIDENT WESSON: The children in the story "The Petrified Creatures" are burned alive.

JIM: It's actually unclear what happens to them.

PRESIDENT WESSON: They die screaming in their beds.

JIM: It's open to interpretation.

LIEUTENANT ERGENBRIGHT: Were either of these stories, *The Petrified Creatures* or *Otto's Coach*, written in the first person?

JIM: *The Petrified Creatures* is.

PRESIDENT WESSON: *(To* LIEUTENANT ERGENBRIGHT*)* *The Petrified Creatures* was not included in Mister McFehren's original authorized syllabus.

JIM: Professors make additions and subtractions to their authorized syllabus all the time.

PRESIDENT WESSON: They shouldn't.

JIM: They do.

PRESIDENT WESSON: They shouldn't. *(Pause. To* LIEUTENANT ERGENBRIGHT*)* I'm sorry, I've interrupted. It's just that what I'm hearing from Mister McFehren is new.

JIM: What's new?

PRESIDENT WESSON: I'm beginning to understand a bit about "how the dominos fell."

JIM: What "dominos"?

PRESIDENT WESSON: It's bewildering.

JIM: It is?

PRESIDENT WESSON: I'm beginning to understand Mister McFehren's teaching methods coupled with the fact that, Mindy — I'm unsure if you're aware of this — but a large part of this situation rests with the fact that Mister McFehren failed to read, before handing out, the stories his students had written.

JIM: A mistake.

PRESIDENT WESSON: He had photocopied all of the work and passed it out, sight unseen. *(To* JIM*)* What was your explanation?

JIM: I admit I made a mistake. *(Beat)* It was a teacher/ trust exercise. *(Beat)* But, President Wesson, I should tell you, and this may be obvious, but in my three years here, Ben Navarro's story is not by any means the first one written in my class which involves this type of premise. Far from it.

PRESIDENT WESSON: Far from it?

JIM: I get two or three a year, if not more.

PRESIDENT WESSON: That's amazing.

JIM: It's not amazing.

PRESIDENT WESSON: It's upsetting.

JIM: The only thing that's *upsetting* is how terrible the writing often is.

PRESIDENT WESSON: Terrible or not, this kind of writing shouldn't be happening at the rate you're describing.

JIM: I'm not describing a rate.

PRESIDENT WESSON: You *are* describing a rate.

JIM: I'm not describing a rate at all.

PRESIDENT WESSON: "Two or three—or more—a year!" That's what you just described!

LIEUTENANT ERGENBRIGHT: Both of you?

PRESIDENT WESSON: Yes?

LIEUTENANT ERGENBRIGHT: If we could stay on point.

PRESIDENT WESSON: We are on point.

LIEUTENANT ERGENBRIGHT: We're getting off point.

PRESIDENT WESSON: We are not off point.

LIEUTENANT ERGENBRIGHT: We are getting off point.

PRESIDENT WESSON: We are staying exactly on point.

LIEUTENANT ERGENBRIGHT: I'd like to finish.

PRESIDENT WESSON: We can be finished right now if you'd like.

LIEUTENANT ERGENBRIGHT: No, no—

PRESIDENT WESSON: We can finish and then, let's see, I'll run over and report our discussion to our board where I'm sure they would love information about all the "mistakes" and they can then couple these mistakes with the previous student and parent complaints about this matter and then they can roll it all together into a festering mass of mistakes and complaints. Coupled along also with this visit to our campus by you. *(Pause)* I'm glad you're here. *(Long pause)* Where was Mister Navarro stationed?

LIEUTENANT ERGENBRIGHT: Baqubah.

PRESIDENT WESSON: Is that a city?

LIEUTENANT ERGENBRIGHT: Yes.

PRESIDENT WESSON: Where is Baqubah?

LIEUTENANT ERGENBRIGHT: Forty-five miles northeast of Baghdad.

PRESIDENT WESSON: Is Baqubah a big city?

LIEUTENANT ERGENBRIGHT: Yes.

PRESIDENT WESSON: How big?

LIEUTENANT ERGENBRIGHT: Probably about three-hundred thousand.

PRESIDENT WESSON: What did Mister Navarro do in Baqubah?

LIEUTENANT ERGENBRIGHT: He helped build floating bridges.

PRESIDENT WESSON: Floating bridges? How many floating bridges did he build?

LIEUTENANT ERGENBRIGHT: One.

PRESIDENT WESSON: Just one?

LIEUTENANT ERGENBRIGHT: Yes.

PRESIDENT WESSON: That's in his file?

LIEUTENANT ERGENBRIGHT: Yes.

PRESIDENT WESSON: Is that classified information? *(Laughs lightly)*

LIEUTENANT ERGENBRIGHT: No. *(Laughs lightly)*

PRESIDENT WESSON: That's not "classified," is it? That he helped build floating bridges? *(Laughs)*

LIEUTENANT ERGENBRIGHT: No.

PRESIDENT WESSON: Is Baqubah a dangerous place?

LIEUTENANT ERGENBRIGHT: It's a war zone.

PRESIDENT WESSON: So yes.

LIEUTENANT ERGENBRIGHT: Yes.

PRESIDENT WESSON: Is Baqubah more dangerous than other places?

LIEUTENANT ERGENBRIGHT: It's seen by some as more unstable than other cities in Iraq so it can be more dangerous as a result.

PRESIDENT WESSON: Why is it unstable?

LIEUTENANT ERGENBRIGHT: It's a war zone.

PRESIDENT WESSON: Have you been to Iraq?

LIEUTENANT ERGENBRIGHT: Yes.

PRESIDENT WESSON: Where in Iraq did you visit?

LIEUTENANT ERGENBRIGHT: Bagdad.

PRESIDENT WESSON: Recently?

LIEUTENANT ERGENBRIGHT: Yes.

PRESIDENT WESSON: Why?

LIEUTENANT ERGENBRIGHT: For my job.

PRESIDENT WESSON: What were you there to do?

LIEUTENANT ERGENBRIGHT: *That's* classified.

JIM: Ben's talked about his time in Iraq.

PRESIDENT WESSON: He talked about Iraq?

JIM: On the first day of class one of Ben's classmates asked him what he did in Iraq and he said that when he got there he and few of his fellow soldiers, right after they landed, got a hold of some old guns, some Iraqi policemen's guns, some old Russian AK-47's and they tried them out, they shot at some piles of old tires.

PRESIDENT WESSON: That's not standard procedure, is it?

LIEUTENANT ERGENBRIGHT: No. *(Pause)* Thank you both so much letting me speak with you. I should go talk to Mister Navarro.

(LIEUTENANT ERGENBRIGHT *crosses to her satchel and begins to put her pen and note pad away.*)

PRESIDENT WESSON: *(To* LIEUTENANT ERGENBRIGHT*)* It would be nice if we had an on-staff psychologist here at Prahl. Our budget can't seem to fit it in currently, but it would be a nice addition.

LIEUTENANT ERGENBRIGHT: I agree.

PRESIDENT WESSON: It certainly would be nice if our staff had the opportunity to refer a student to an on-staff psychologist.

JIM: Not that I would do that.

PRESIDENT WESSON: But you could if we could afford to procure an on-staff psychologist.

JIM: I wouldn't tell a student that he or she should go get his or her brain checked just because he or she did something someone didn't like.

(A beat)

LIEUTENANT ERGENBRIGHT: The main reason I agreed with President Wesson is that without an on-staff psychologist there doesn't seem to be a clear outlet for interior expression.

JIM: There are many outlets at this school for interior expression.

LIEUTENANT ERGENBRIGHT: Few besides the artistic is my point.

JIM: What?

LIEUTENANT ERGENBRIGHT: —I'm sorry—

JIM: Art is not an acceptable outlet for interior discussion?

LIEUTENANT ERGENBRIGHT: That's not what I meant.

JIM: A psychologist is just better trained.

LIEUTENANT ERGENBRIGHT: No. Please. I'm not attempting to give advice. I'm only agreeing that an on-staff psychologist would be useful.

PRESIDENT WESSON: It would be useful.

LIEUTENANT ERGENBRIGHT: It would aid in a situation such as this one.

JIM: Ben's situation.

LIEUTENANT ERGENBRIGHT: Yes.

JIM: Ben is fine. Ben is just your basic, normal, twenty-two year-old kid.

(A beat)

LIEUTENANT ERGENBRIGHT: So was that a problem?

JIM: Was what a problem?

LIEUTENANT ERGENBRIGHT: Are your "normal" students the ones which tend to create "hokum from the common stack?"

JIM: No, bad writers create "hokum from the common stack."

LIEUTENANT ERGENBRIGHT: So does "normal" equal bad?

JIM: Not always.

PRESIDENT WESSON: *(To* LIEUTENANT ERGENBRIGHT*)* When you're through, would it be possible to let me have a copy of your findings?

LIEUTENANT ERGENBRIGHT: I'm sorry, that will be private.

PRESIDENT WESSON: I would like to know if you think there might be problems.

JIM: President Wesson, there are no problems.

PRESIDENT WESSON: *(To* JIM*)* You just told us a bit ago that Mr. Navarro fired an Iraqi policeman's gun.

JIM: So?

PRESIDENT WESSON: We don't know a thing about him.

JIM: What do you need to know?

PRESIDENT WESSON: Obviously something is going on.

JIM: Nothing is going on!

PRESIDENT WESSON: There is a lot going on. If Mister Navarro is suffering from something, some kind of posttraumatic stress—

JIM: —please—

PRESIDENT WESSON: — or if your teaching methods—

JIM: —my "methods" —?

PRESIDENT WESSON: — perhaps if you'd considered attending one of the new faculty training seminars—

JIM: I'm not new faculty!

PRESIDENT WESSON: You neglected to attend the seminar when you were first hired—

JIM: So what?

PRESIDENT WESSON: A seminar may be helpful—

JIM: I've had nearly ten years experience with undergrads—

PRESIDENT WESSON: Mullen College?

JIM: Yes.

PRESIDENT WESSON: That just barely qualifies—

JIM: Mullen barely qualifies?

PRESIDENT WESSON: —west coast schools—

JIM: —west coast schools —?

PRESIDENT WESSON: —strong qualifications are an asset—

JIM: — I know they are—

PRESIDENT WESSON: —strong qualifications are an asset—!

JIM: — I have strong qualifications —!

PRESIDENT WESSON: Then you should know something more about Mister Navarro!

JIM: With all due respect, President Wesson, every goddamn horseshit opinion you have of Ben is based solely on a few pages of idiotic nonsense written for some low-level throwaway fiction writing class!

(A pause)

PRESIDENT WESSON: Horseshit opinion?

JIM: Yes.

PRESIDENT WESSON: I have a horseshit opinion regarding an alarming student-written first person narrative detailing a young woman's exceedingly brutal kidnapping, rape and murder?

JIM: Yes.

(A pause)

PRESIDENT WESSON: My opinion isn't horseshit—

JIM: — I got worked up, I'm sorry—

PRESIDENT WESSON: — and Mr. McFehren, if you believe you teach a "throwaway fiction writing class," we need to have a future discussion of what classes of yours you deem worthwhile.

JIM: All my classes are worthwhile. I was worked up. I didn't mean to say "horseshit".

(A pause)

PRESIDENT WESSON: I believe we'd finished?

LIEUTENANT ERGENBRIGHT: Yes.

PRESIDENT WESSON: I'll have my assistant call Mr. Navarro for you to make sure he's at home.

LIEUTENANT ERGENBRIGHT: Thank you.

PRESIDENT WESSON: If you need to speak to me again, just phone my extension. Jean can give you a card with my extension number and we can talk, in person or on the telephone. I'm afraid Mr. McFehren has students and classes to attend to, so he won't be available to talk but you can speak with me or Provost Overton or both of us together, that would be fine, that we can arrange.

(LIEUTENANT ERGENBRIGHT *stands, extending her hand to* PRESIDENT WESSON. LIEUTENANT ERGENBRIGHT *and* PRESIDENT WESSON *shake hands.)*

LIEUTENANT ERGENBRIGHT: Thank you.

PRESIDENT WESSON: Have Jean get you Mr. Navarro's number. She'll also be happy to supply you with a map of the campus so you don't get lost going to his room. Not that you would get lost, you found my office just fine, but a map is always good.

LIEUTENANT ERGENBRIGHT: I agree.

PRESIDENT WESSON: Good.

LIEUTENANT ERGENBRIGHT: *(Turning to* JIM*)* Thank you, Jim.

JIM: Sure.

PRESIDENT WESSON: *(To* LIEUTENANT ERGENBRIGHT*)* I would really like us to get together and speak for sure at least once before you go back to Georgia for good.

LIEUTENANT ERGENBRIGHT: If I have time.

PRESIDENT WESSON: Just to say goodbye.

(LIEUTENANT ERGENBRIGHT *nods. She then picks up her satchel, crosses to the door, opens it and exits. A pause.* PRESIDENT WESSON *sits.)*

PRESIDENT WESSON: Do you have a cell phone?

JIM: Yes.

PRESIDENT WESSON: Please keep it turned on.

JIM: Okay.

PRESIDENT WESSON: Leave the number with Jean.

JIM: Okay.

PRESIDENT WESSON: Thank you.

(A pause. JIM *stands. He exits, shutting the door behind him.)*

(Lights fade to black.)

END ACT ONE

ACT TWO

(Lights up on PRESIDENT WESSON's *office. It is early afternoon, four days later.* LIEUTENANT ERGENBRIGHT, *in dress casual attire, sits on one of the chairs, the door to the office open. She has left a small rolling suitcase near the door and her satchel is on the floor near her feet. She waits.)*

*(*PRESIDENT WESSON, *in slightly older clothes, enters. He shuts the door behind him.)*

PRESIDENT WESSON: Hello.

LIEUTENANT ERGENBRIGHT: Hello.

PRESIDENT WESSON: When is your flight out?

LIEUTENANT ERGENBRIGHT: Soon.

PRESIDENT WESSON: Have you had lunch yet?

LIEUTENANT ERGENBRIGHT: No, not yet.

PRESIDENT WESSON: Were you just going to grab a bite on the airplane?

LIEUTENANT ERGENBRIGHT: I thought I would.

PRESIDENT WESSON: Airplane food lunch?

LIEUTENANT ERGENBRIGHT: Yes.

PRESIDENT WESSON: What sort of lunch is that?

LIEUTENANT ERGENBRIGHT: I don't mind.

PRESIDENT WESSON: Let me have some lunch brought over instead.

LIEUTENANT ERGENBRIGHT: That's all right.

PRESIDENT WESSON: Would you like a pita pocket? There's a pita pocket place close by. I can have Jean run over and get us both each a pita pocket.

LIEUTENANT ERGENBRIGHT: That's all right, I had a late breakfast.

PRESIDENT WESSON: You did? What did you have?

LIEUTENANT ERGENBRIGHT: I bought a bagel at the student union.

PRESIDENT WESSON: Did you happen to get some coffee from the student union?

LIEUTENANT ERGENBRIGHT: Yes.

PRESIDENT WESSON: From that little stand by the stairs?

LIEUTENANT ERGENBRIGHT: I did.

PRESIDENT WESSON: Isn't that some good coffee? It's strong coffee. Strong morning coffee for the sleepy college student. I have a cup, *(Shuffles a few things around on his desk)* here it is, *(Finds a cup)* this cup. A refill cup. When I use this cup, I get a discount — half off. But it seems I don't really need this cup. They always fill it for free. I can get you a free coffee, too, if you'd like, if you'd like some more coffee.

LIEUTENANT ERGENBRIGHT: This morning's was all I needed.

PRESIDENT WESSON: Because it was so strong?

LIEUTENANT ERGENBRIGHT: I can't drink more than one cup a day.

PRESIDENT WESSON: Is that right?

LIEUTENANT ERGENBRIGHT: Yes.

PRESIDENT WESSON: No coffee for you in the afternoon?

LIEUTENANT ERGENBRIGHT: No.

PRESIDENT WESSON: Why's that?

LIEUTENANT ERGENBRIGHT: I'd be up all night.

PRESIDENT WESSON: You would?

LIEUTENANT ERGENBRIGHT: Yes.

PRESIDENT WESSON: Caffeine does nothing to me whatsoever.

LIEUTENANT ERGENBRIGHT: You're lucky.

PRESIDENT WESSON: No, I wish it did. I can drink coffee whenever I like and I still can fall asleep at the drop of a hat. In front of the television, zonk and I'm out in the middle of whatever is on. Eight-thirty—nine o'clock, I start bobbing, my mouth hanging open and then I'm out, good-night. My poor wife. She gets so annoyed with me. One time I fell asleep in front of the television and my grandson put a rubber "superball" in my mouth. I nearly choked to death on it!

LIEUTENANT ERGENBRIGHT: That's awful.

PRESIDENT WESSON: It wasn't awful. He was just playing. It wasn't dangerous. I woke up. I spit the ball out. I was fine. It was nothing. It was just a ball. *(Pause)* So, how are you, then? Did you get to see any other parts of the campus?

LIEUTENANT ERGENBRIGHT: I stopped by your library.

PRESIDENT WESSON: Students sometimes sleep in the library and we have to have other students in charge of waking them up and booting them out. Did you see any sleeping students?

LIEUTENANT ERGENBRIGHT: No.

PRESIDENT WESSON: They stick to the corners and dark areas of the library so they're hard to spot. Did you happen to visit anywhere else?

LIEUTENANT ERGENBRIGHT: I didn't get a chance.

PRESIDENT WESSON: We have some nice shops just off of campus. There's a nice jewelry store called "Doane's Jewelers." My wife and I purchased our wedding rings from them almost thirty-five years ago. We still take the rings there to get cleaned every year. I also purchased my watch there.

LIEUTENANT ERGENBRIGHT: I was at the dorm most of the time.

PRESIDENT WESSON: Good.

LIEUTENANT ERGENBRIGHT: His building is very nice.

PRESIDENT WESSON: That's new, it was built only two years ago. "Heideman Hall." Did you get to see the student lounge?

LIEUTENANT ERGENBRIGHT: Yes.

PRESIDENT WESSON: It's a bit fancy.

LIEUTENANT ERGENBRIGHT: It seemed comfortable.

PRESIDENT WESSON: It's very popular. I've seen it so crowded that not one more person could study in there unless they wanted to spread out on the floor.

LIEUTENANT ERGENBRIGHT: We had lunch together one day in the cafeteria.

PRESIDENT WESSON: You mean the dining hall?

LIEUTENANT ERGENBRIGHT: Yes.

PRESIDENT WESSON: You should have seen the old dining hall. It was inefficient and small. How was the food?

LIEUTENANT ERGENBRIGHT: Very good.

PRESIDENT WESSON: I'd hope so.

LIEUTENANT ERGENBRIGHT: I remember eating in the dorms when I was in school. We had one meal we called, "Vein Burgers."

PRESIDENT WESSON: Hamburgers?

LIEUTENANT ERGENBRIGHT: We called them "Vein Burgers."

PRESIDENT WESSON: Because the meat was questionable?

LIEUTENANT ERGENBRIGHT: Yes.

PRESIDENT WESSON: "Vein Burgers."

LIEUTENANT ERGENBRIGHT: They tasted pretty awful.

PRESIDENT WESSON: But you ate them anyway, didn't you?

LIEUTENANT ERGENBRIGHT: We did.

PRESIDENT WESSON: Students will eat anything. *(Beat)* It's good that you had some nice downtime.

LIEUTENANT ERGENBRIGHT: We were able to spend quite a lot of time together.

PRESIDENT WESSON: And he's feeling better?

LIEUTENANT ERGENBRIGHT: He's feeling all right.

PRESIDENT WESSON: I spoke with him on the telephone.

LIEUTENANT ERGENBRIGHT: I know.

PRESIDENT WESSON: The day before yesterday.

LIEUTENANT ERGENBRIGHT: He told me you'd called him.

PRESIDENT WESSON: He was a bit tense.

LIEUTENANT ERGENBRIGHT: More frazzled than anything.

PRESIDENT WESSON: "Frazzled?" Is that a psychological term? "Frazzled"? Is that your diagnosis? *(Laughs)*

LIEUTENANT ERGENBRIGHT: *(Lightly laughs)* No. It's not.

PRESIDENT WESSON: He's "frazzled?"

LIEUTENANT ERGENBRIGHT: That's not my diagnosis, no.

PRESIDENT WESSON: That he's "frazzled?"

LIEUTENANT ERGENBRIGHT: He's stressed.

PRESIDENT WESSON: He's stressed.

LIEUTENANT ERGENBRIGHT: He's mostly stressed, this being his first semester.

PRESIDENT WESSON: The article in the campus paper must not have helped.

LIEUTENANT ERGENBRIGHT: No.

PRESIDENT WESSON: He won't be speaking to them, will he?

LIEUTENANT ERGENBRIGHT: No.

PRESIDENT WESSON: He's not going to talk with them?

LIEUTENANT ERGENBRIGHT: He's quite embarrassed.

PRESIDENT WESSON: Yes.

LIEUTENANT ERGENBRIGHT: There's actually something I wanted to speak to you about before I leave—

PRESIDENT WESSON: What is it?

LIEUTENANT ERGENBRIGHT: If I could speak to you about what Ben is feeling.

PRESIDENT WESSON: You'd said before that was private.

LIEUTENANT ERGENBRIGHT: But if I can somehow say anything to help ease things for him, I would very much like to do so.

PRESIDENT WESSON: What would you need to ease?

LIEUTENANT ERGENBRIGHT: I won't tell you anything that's private, just some thoughts.

PRESIDENT WESSON: all right.

LIEUTENANT ERGENBRIGHT: Just for a moment.

PRESIDENT WESSON: That's fine.

LIEUTENANT ERGENBRIGHT: all right.

PRESIDENT WESSON: Go ahead.

(A pause)

LIEUTENANT ERGENBRIGHT: I would only like to mention just, after speaking with Ben these past few days, after he and I have spoken to each other, my view is that Ben is something of an introvert—

PRESIDENT WESSON: He's shy.

LIEUTENANT ERGENBRIGHT: Yes, but, even so, Ben has opened up to me. He harbors many emotions, emotions he's trying seriously to understand. He's having a somewhat difficult time with a few of his classes—

PRESIDENT WESSON: —yes—

LIEUTENANT ERGENBRIGHT: —and as you said, you spoke to Ben on the telephone—

PRESIDENT WESSON: —he was a bit tense—

LIEUTENANT ERGENBRIGHT: — he's nervous—

PRESIDENT WESSON: —regarding —?

LIEUTENANT ERGENBRIGHT: —his continuance—

PRESIDENT WESSON: —his continuance—?

LIEUTENANT ERGENBRIGHT: Ben had some feelings that when you spoke with him that perhaps you believe he should look at other campuses.

PRESIDENT WESSON: I don't necessarily believe that.

LIEUTENANT ERGENBRIGHT: Did you suggest he take some time off?

PRESIDENT WESSON: I only wanted to show him he had a number of options.

LIEUTENANT ERGENBRIGHT: Options including leaving?

PRESIDENT WESSON: I suppose that I suggested that as an option, among others.

LIEUTENANT ERGENBRIGHT: I believe that may have not helped, you giving him that option.

PRESIDENT WESSON: I only mentioned to Mister Navarro that if he would like to take a break, just for awhile, that would be fine.

LIEUTENANT ERGENBRIGHT: He doesn't want to take a break.

PRESIDENT WESSON: It could be a good thing.

LIEUTENANT ERGENBRIGHT: I don't think it could.

(A pause)

PRESIDENT WESSON: When I was enrolled here at Prahl—I've never told anyone this before, actually, no one but my wife really knows about this—but when I was enrolled here at Prahl I was overwhelmed a bit and I took a break, a semester break. It was my sophomore year. I traveled to Spain. It was wonderful.

LIEUTENANT ERGENBRIGHT: I don't think Ben wants to go to Spain.

PRESIDENT WESSON: I'm not suggesting he go to Spain, I'm only suggesting that breaks are sometimes necessary.

LIEUTENANT ERGENBRIGHT: He only wants to stay in school.

PRESIDENT WESSON: Spain was good for me, that's what I was saying. It helped me refocus and come back with a new-found energy.

LIEUTENANT ERGENBRIGHT: Ben told me he felt he had made a mistake.

PRESIDENT WESSON: Is that right?

LIEUTENANT ERGENBRIGHT: Yes.

PRESIDENT WESSON: He told you he felt he made a mistake?

LIEUTENANT ERGENBRIGHT: Yes.

PRESIDENT WESSON: He *has* made a mistake.

LIEUTENANT ERGENBRIGHT: He understands he has.

PRESIDENT WESSON: He does?

LIEUTENANT ERGENBRIGHT: He agrees.

PRESIDENT WESSON: He agrees?

LIEUTENANT ERGENBRIGHT: He's shy, as you've said.

PRESIDENT WESSON: Yes.

LIEUTENANT ERGENBRIGHT: His modes of expression are a little confused. He didn't mean to cause problems and agrees he should try harder to express himself in a better way. He feels that after his sessions with me, he now has the courage to seek further treatment on his own for any adjustment problems he may be having.

PRESIDENT WESSON: That's good.

LIEUTENANT ERGENBRIGHT: But he wishes to stay in school.

PRESIDENT WESSON: I see.

LIEUTENANT ERGENBRIGHT: Perhaps you could speak with him again?

PRESIDENT WESSON: On the telephone?

LIEUTENANT ERGENBRIGHT: On the telephone or perhaps you could meet him for coffee. He would like that.

PRESIDENT WESSON: That may be all right.

LIEUTENANT ERGENBRIGHT: He'd appreciate your time.

PRESIDENT WESSON: Perhaps I could meet him for coffee.

LIEUTENANT ERGENBRIGHT: That would be helpful.

PRESIDENT WESSON: At the student union?

LIEUTENANT ERGENBRIGHT: Whereever you'd like.

(A pause. PRESIDENT WESSON'S *telephone buzzes. It startles him for a moment, and he then picks up the receiver.)*

PRESIDENT WESSON: *(Into telephone)* Yes? No. I'll speak with him later.

*(*JIM *opens the door to the office, sticking his head in the doorway. His clothes are nearly identical to previous, only perhaps a bit more pressed. He carries a manila envelope.)*

JIM: Hi.

PRESIDENT WESSON: *(Into telephone)* It's all right. No, Jean, it's all right.

JIM: If I could come in, for just a moment, just to say goodbye and drop something off.

PRESIDENT WESSON: *(Hangs up receiver)* Hello.

JIM: I heard Lieutenant Ergenbright was leaving today.

PRESIDENT WESSON: Yes.

JIM: Is it okay if I come in?

PRESIDENT WESSON: It's fine.

JIM: This isn't a problem?

PRESIDENT WESSON: No. Come in.

*(*JIM *enters the room. He stands near the door.)*

PRESIDENT WESSON: If you could leave the door open.

*(*JIM *puts a hand on the door.)*

PRESIDENT WESSON: Swing it half-way.

*(*JIM *swings the door half-way open. A pause.)*

JIM: Hello.

PRESIDENT WESSON: Lieutenant Ergenbright only has a short time before her flight.

LIEUTENANT ERGENBRIGHT: Hello, Jim.

JIM: She'd requested a copy of my short story. *(To* LIEUTENANT ERGENBRIGHT*)* Here you go.

LIEUTENANT ERGENBRIGHT: Thank you.

JIM: I didn't forget.

*(*JIM *hands* LIEUTENANT ERGENBRIGHT *the manila envelope.* LIEUTENANT ERGENBRIGHT *opens the envelope and removes the short story.)*

LIEUTENANT ERGENBRIGHT: Thanks.

JIM: *Bicentennial Saucer.*

LIEUTENANT ERGENBRIGHT: I very much look forward to reading it.

JIM: Great.

LIEUTENANT ERGENBRIGHT: Thank you very much.

JIM: No problem.

*(*LIEUTENANT ERGENBRIGHT *looks over the manuscript for a moment.)*

LIEUTENANT ERGENBRIGHT: Jim. This is going to sound silly.

JIM: What will sound silly?

LIEUTENANT ERGENBRIGHT: Okay, well. I was wondering if you could, if you wouldn't mind autographing your story for me?

JIM: Autographing it?

LIEUTENANT ERGENBRIGHT: Yes.

JIM: Oh. Well. Sure. Okay.

LIEUTENANT ERGENBRIGHT: Since I was a kid I've collected autographs, famous people's autographs.

(LIEUTENANT ERGENBRIGHT *picks up her satchel and finds her pen. She hands it to* JIM.)

JIM: I'm not famous. *(Beat)* Do you want me to write, "To Mindy?"

LIEUTENANT ERGENBRIGHT: Just your autograph is fine.

JIM: Okay. *(He signs the short story.)* There you go.

(JIM *hands the pen back to* LIEUTENANT ERGENBRIGHT. LIEUTENANT ERGENBRIGHT *returns the pen to her satchel and places the story back into the envelope.)*

LIEUTENANT ERGENBRIGHT: You must both think I'm a big goof.

JIM: You're not a big goof.

LIEUTENANT ERGENBRIGHT: You should have seen me a few years ago when I was in Los Angeles. I was like a tiger on the prowl. A big goofus tiger.

(LIEUTENANT ERGENBRIGHT *places the envelope in her satchel.)*

JIM: Did you get anyone's autograph in Los Angeles?

LIEUTENANT ERGENBRIGHT: I tried but failed miserably.

PRESIDENT WESSON: Did you visit Hollywood Boulevard?

LIEUTENANT ERGENBRIGHT: Yes.

PRESIDENT WESSON: *(To* JIM*)* Is that all you needed?

JIM: *(To* LIEUTENANT ERGENBRIGHT*)* How did things go with Ben?

LIEUTENANT ERGENBRIGHT: Very well.

JIM: The two of you got along well?

LIEUTENANT ERGENBRIGHT: Yes.

JIM: He's not the most outgoing person, as you I'm sure realized.

LIEUTENANT ERGENBRIGHT: Yes.

PRESIDENT WESSON: Jim?

JIM: *(To* LIEUTENANT ERGENBRIGHT*)* Actually, I was wondering, if you have a minute, if you wouldn't mind, I was wondering if you wouldn't mind if I asked you a quick question.

LIEUTENANT ERGENBRIGHT: Sure.

JIM: Just something quick.

LIEUTENANT ERGENBRIGHT: It's no problem. Please go ahead.

JIM: May I sit? *(A pause. He sits.)*

PRESIDENT WESSON: Please don't sit.

JIM: I'll only be sitting a moment.

PRESIDENT WESSON: We're nearly through.

JIM: I only have a quick question. I'll only be a moment.

PRESIDENT WESSON: You don't need to sit.

JIM: I'm already sitting.

PRESIDENT WESSON: Then please make it quick.

JIM: I wanted to ask you Mindy about something Ben had also mentioned the same time he mentioned to my class he had mentioned firing that Iraqi gun. Something I neglected to bring up at the time I spoke about what he'd said. I wanted to ask about something he also told us which had also happened. He told us a few other things, he mentioned to us that he had witnessed a few things, that he'd seen some things that had bothered him, that he'd seen a number of killings. *(Beat)* He told us that while he was in Iraq he'd witnessed a Humvee accident involving three men, all of which were killed, and that he'd also seen a fire-fight from a short distance and they'd brought the wounded soldiers into the building he was guarding and he saw one of the soldiers that had been killed — slaughtered, he had said — slaughtered very badly and missing half of his face and most of his lower body. He'd told us that lately he'd been dreaming of the dead men, that he often dreamed especially of the murdered and slaughtered soldier, the soldier missing half his face and most of his body.

LIEUTENANT ERGENBRIGHT: I'm confused.

PRESIDENT WESSON: Ben spoke about these incidents in your class?

JIM: He did.

PRESIDENT WESSON: He told the class that he dreamed about slaughtered soldiers?

JIM: Yes.

LIEUTENANT ERGENBRIGHT: What is the question here, Jim?

PRESIDENT WESSON: *(To* LIEUTENANT ERGENBRIGHT*)* Mindy — did Mr. Navarro witness these incidents?

LIEUTENANT ERGENBRIGHT: Did he witness them?

PRESIDENT WESSON: Did he mention these incidents to you when you spoke to him?

LIEUTENANT ERGENBRIGHT: I'm sorry, but I can't discuss what specifics Ben and I spoke about.

(A pause. PRESIDENT WESSON *stands and shuts the door.)*

PRESIDENT WESSON: I'm just shutting that.

*(*PRESIDENT WESSON *returns to his seat.)*

PRESIDENT WESSON: What Mister McFehren is telling us sounds like a few disturbing scenarios.

LIEUTENANT ERGENBRIGHT: I'm sure it does.

PRESIDENT WESSON: And you can't deny or confirm any of it?

LIEUTENANT ERGENBRIGHT: I'm sure both of you are aware that all soldiers involved in a conflict may, at one time or another, see casualties first-hand.

PRESIDENT WESSON: Of course.

LIEUTENANT ERGENBRIGHT: Then take Jim's description of what Mister Navarro spoke about for only what it is.

PRESIDENT WESSON: Did Mister Navarro mention to you he was having dreams about dead soldiers?

LIEUTENANT ERGENBRIGHT: I already told you I can't discuss it.

PRESIDENT WESSON: You can't give us a yes or no?

LIEUTENANT ERGENBRIGHT: I can't.

PRESIDENT WESSON: You can't talk about facts?

LIEUTENANT ERGENBRIGHT: I can't discuss private conversations.

JIM: I'm sorry, Mindy, but my question I wanted ask you wasn't regarding the incidents Ben had seen. I had a question about something else.

LIEUTENANT ERGENBRIGHT: All right.

JIM: I brought up what he said in order to illustrate my question.

LIEUTENANT ERGENBRIGHT: All right.

JIM: In order for my question to be understood in context.

LIEUTENANT ERGENBRIGHT: Ask your question.

JIM: I wanted to ask if you believe Ben was perhaps previously inclined.

LIEUTENANT ERGENBRIGHT: Previously inclined?

JIM: If you think Ben could have had a predilection for this sort of thing. If he might have, had he been in some other writing class, if he might have written the same story for another professor. What's your professional opinion?

LIEUTENANT ERGENBRIGHT: I don't think I wish to offer one, I'm sorry.

JIM: You don't wish to offer one?

LIEUTENANT ERGENBRIGHT: No, I'm sorry.

JIM: Why not?

LIEUTENANT ERGENBRIGHT: Why do you need my professional opinion?

JIM: I just want your opinion.

LIEUTENANT ERGENBRIGHT: You don't need to know my opinion.

JIM: It would be useful.

LIEUTENANT ERGENBRIGHT: It's not really important to anything currently involving Ben.

JIM: I'm sorry, but I disagree.

PRESIDENT WESSON: I think Mister McFehren might be right. Let's hear your opinion.

LIEUTENANT ERGENBRIGHT: No.

PRESIDENT WESSON: Give us your opinion.

LIEUTENANT ERGENBRIGHT: I don't have one.

PRESIDENT WESSON: Conjecture, then.

LIEUTENANT ERGENBRIGHT: I don't conjecture.

PRESIDENT WESSON: I doubt that's true. (Beat) What's your opinion? Tell us your opinion. Given what Mister McFehren described to us and after your chats with Mister Navarro, would he have written the story on his own anyway? You'd agree, this is a valid query, one which you, Lieutenant, can help to illuminate. You told me you had many deep conversations with him, you told me you'd spent lots of time alone with

him discussing all sorts of matters and you also
boasted that you and he had made a strong, personal
connection, one which gave you clear insight into who
he is and how he feels. So with your new knowledge,
give us your opinion. Given your education and
experience, you are more the expert than we. Given
your secret conversations with him, you are the one
more in the know.

(A pause)

LIEUTENANT ERGENBRIGHT: You want my opinion.

PRESIDENT WESSON: Your professional opinion.

LIEUTENANT ERGENBRIGHT: My opinion, I suppose, is
that I don't think that Ben would have written that
story if Mister McFehren hadn't been his professor.

JIM: Wait—

LIEUTENANT ERGENBRIGHT: If Mister McFehren hadn't
prompted Ben, I don't believe he would have written
that story at all.

JIM: I didn't prompt him!

LIEUTENANT ERGENBRIGHT: You wanted my opinion.

JIM: I didn't prompt Ben. I didn't know he had
emotional problems.

LIEUTENANT ERGENBRIGHT: He doesn't have emotional
problems.

JIM: He has a difficult time communicating.

LIEUTENANT ERGENBRIGHT: That's not an "emotional
problem."

JIM: I didn't prompt him.

LIEUTENANT ERGENBRIGHT: He told me you had.

JIM: How did I prompt him?

LIEUTENANT ERGENBRIGHT: He said you encouraged him.

JIM: So you're saying that his entire story was my idea?

LIEUTENANT ERGENBRIGHT: That's not what I'm saying.

JIM: You're saying this whole thing; the blood, the screams, the electrical wires, the forced oral sex, he got all that from me?

LIEUTENANT ERGENBRIGHT: I'm not saying that at all.

JIM: Because you never hear about anything like that happening with the army — nothing like that going on with Uncle Sam's Regiment, never never.

(A pause)

LIEUTENANT ERGENBRIGHT: Are you attempting to get something across?

JIM: I am, yes.

LIEUTENANT ERGENBRIGHT: What is it you're attempting?

JIM: To clear the air.

LIEUTENANT ERGENBRIGHT: What air do you think you're clearing?

JIM: You have no idea what's going on with Ben.

LIEUTENANT ERGENBRIGHT: And you do?

JIM: I would think so.

LIEUTENANT ERGENBRIGHT: You're very off base.

JIM: Am I?

LIEUTENANT ERGENBRIGHT: Ben has a strong imagination.

JIM: I know that.

LIEUTENANT ERGENBRIGHT: An imagination which did not need your style of encouragement.

JIM: I treated him as I would any other student. It was a writing class so he had to write.

LIEUTENANT ERGENBRIGHT: I've read his other writing and none of it reads like *An Unpracticed Correction*.

JIM: I know that.

LIEUTENANT ERGENBRIGHT: He told me he'd written the story after speaking with you one-on-one.

JIM: I only told him he needed to dig deeper than his previous stories he'd written for me about his grandmother and some lousy high-stakes poker game.

LIEUTENANT ERGENBRIGHT: You did more than encourage a story-line change.

JIM: Not really, no.

LIEUTENANT ERGENBRIGHT: You told him you wanted more.

(A beat)

JIM: My contract may not be renewed for next year.

LIEUTENANT ERGENBRIGHT: I'm sorry.

PRESIDENT WESSON: We review all adjunct contracts at the end of each academic year.

JIM: I've been suspended.

PRESIDENT WESSON: For evaluation purposes only. *(Pause)* Perhaps we should be more aware of the affects of a student's military service. Perhaps psychological pre-screening of former soldiers should be a part of the student application process.

LIEUTENANT ERGENBRIGHT: I disagree.

PRESIDENT WESSON: You don't believe a psychological evaluation would be beneficial?

JIM: What about in specific cases?

LIEUTENANT ERGENBRIGHT: Specific cases?

JIM: I'm sure you would agree there are certainly soldiers who need some kind of evaluation before returning to civilian life.

PRESIDENT WESSON: Yes, war can create psychic damage, that is a clear fact.

JIM: And the trauma of returning home takes a toll.

PRESIDENT WESSON: It's a very combustible mix.

JIM: I imagine a person's mind would turn sharply in all sorts of directions when confronting the differences between battlefield and home life.

PRESIDENT WESSON: Perhaps a psychologist's more direct participation *during* engagement would be of better use—

JIM: — I'm sure that's done, isn't it —?

PRESIDENT WESSON: —to discuss coping with life after being exposed to the trauma of war—

JIM: —to make sure one is prepared for a changed relationship with his or her surroundings—

PRESIDENT WESSON: —to understand there could be risk—

JIM: —to understand the possibility of risk—

PRESIDENT WESSON: —to make sure all dangerous aspects of personality are thoroughly examined and rooted out—

LIEUTENANT ERGENBRIGHT: Or perhaps the more appropriate action would be a psychological examination of the staff of this intrusive, impersonal and paranoid little school. *(Long pause)* I apologize.

JIM: It's all right.

PRESIDENT WESSON: I'm troubled that you were sent here to speak with one of my students.

LIEUTENANT ERGENBRIGHT: I was sent to speak with one of our soldiers.

PRESIDENT WESSON: Which did you try to help? The soldier or the student?

LIEUTENANT ERGENBRIGHT: I'm really very sorry I said what I said.

JIM: It's really all right.

LIEUTENANT ERGENBRIGHT: I truly believe Ben presents no danger to this school.

PRESIDENT WESSON: I've had students get into a variety of trouble here at Prahl. I've had students tie other students to trees. I've had students climb over the rail of the pedestrian bridge and jump fifteen feet to the river below. I've had students caught having sex in the cemetery.

LIEUTENANT ERGENBRIGHT: Ben's an introvert.

PRESIDENT WESSON: Isolation breeds contempt.

LIEUTENANT ERGENBRIGHT: Not in his case.

PRESIDENT WESSON: Please stop pouring blood into the water.

LIEUTENANT ERGENBRIGHT: How am I "pouring blood into the water?"

PRESIDENT WESSON: Through your blinded eyes and weakened sense of right and wrong.

LIEUTENANT ERGENBRIGHT: That's outrageous, really.

PRESIDENT WESSON: You're stirring up the chum.

LIEUTENANT ERGENBRIGHT: I've spoken to Ben—

PRESIDENT WESSON: — exactly my point—

LIEUTENANT ERGENBRIGHT: I've spoken to Ben a great deal—

PRESIDENT WESSON: And you're telling us he has no strong emotions?

LIEUTENANT ERGENBRIGHT: Yes, he has strong emotions.

PRESIDENT WESSON: He's not the "gentle robot" you describe?

LIEUTENANT ERGENBRIGHT: I never described him as a "gentle robot."

JIM: He's emotional.

LIEUTENANT ERGENBRIGHT: Actually, he's very much the opposite. It's difficult to pry emotions from a person who has recently been trained to turn away from them.

PRESIDENT WESSON: That's your job, to force him to examine his emotions.

LIEUTENANT ERGENBRIGHT: I'm not here to force anyone to do anything—

PRESIDENT WESSON: But you found examining his emotions "difficult."

LIEUTENANT ERGENBRIGHT: I was speaking generally about returning soldiers when I used the word "difficult."

PRESIDENT WESSON: You were generalizing?

LIEUTENANT ERGENBRIGHT: — only when describing returning soldiers—

PRESIDENT WESSON: So Mister Navarro's closed himself off?

LIEUTENANT ERGENBRIGHT: No—

PRESIDENT WESSON: He's over-expressive?

LIEUTENANT ERGENBRIGHT: No.

PRESIDENT WESSON: He's a well-balanced individual on all counts?

LIEUTENANT ERGENBRIGHT: No.

PRESIDENT WESSON: Then what is happening?

LIEUTENANT ERGENBRIGHT: I thought we had an understanding.

PRESIDENT WESSON: When?

LIEUTENANT ERGENBRIGHT: I thought you had agreed you would talk with him.

PRESIDENT WESSON: I said I may think about speaking with him.

LIEUTENANT ERGENBRIGHT: Over coffee, you said you would consider it.

JIM: Ben and President Wesson are getting coffee?

LIEUTENANT ERGENBRIGHT: (*To* PRESIDENT WESSON) If you are confused about Ben's emotional state, then the best way to learn is to sit down with him.

PRESIDENT WESSON: I don't know if that's possible.

LIEUTENANT ERGENBRIGHT: Please let him tell you himself his own perspective.

PRESIDENT WESSON: His behavior and his story have spoken very loudly already.

LIEUTENANT ERGENBRIGHT: I understand.

PRESIDENT WESSON: And your involvement has clouded this issue even further.

(*A beat*)

LIEUTENANT ERGENBRIGHT: Yes.

PRESIDENT WESSON: He would have much explaining to do.

LIEUTENANT ERGENBRIGHT: He would answer any question you may have, I'm sure.

PRESIDENT WESSON: He'll have to come down to the office instead of coffee. He'll have to come here, I'll have to meet with him here.

LIEUTENANT ERGENBRIGHT: I'm sure that would not be a problem.

PRESIDENT WESSON: It would just be he and I, no coffee.

LIEUTENANT ERGENBRIGHT: A serious discussion regarding the facts at hand.

PRESIDENT WESSON: Yes.

LIEUTENANT ERGENBRIGHT: I think that would be wise and appropriate.

JIM: Ben will be coming here?

PRESIDENT WESSON: Yes.

JIM: You'll be speaking with him alone?

PRESIDENT WESSON: Of course.

JIM: I think it may be better if I were here, too.

PRESIDENT WESSON: You will not be at that meeting, Mister McFehren.

JIM: It might be better if I were. To help you. *(Beat)* Ben's been acting out.

PRESIDENT WESSON: He's been "acting out?"

JIM: He's been roaming the campus.

PRESIDENT WESSON: He's been "roaming the campus?"

JIM: At night, for the past few nights, he's been roaming the campus.

LIEUTENANT ERGENBRIGHT: What?

PRESIDENT WESSON: He told you he was roaming the campus at night?

JIM: Yes.

PRESIDENT WESSON: When did he tell you?

JIM: He called me at home yesterday. He said he had been having a difficult time speaking with Mindy, so he asked if he and I could talk. He said he needed a friend. Someone he could trust.

LIEUTENANT ERGENBRIGHT: You?

PRESIDENT WESSON: Was he having trouble sleeping?

JIM: Ben hurt a female student.

PRESIDENT WESSON: He did what?

LIEUTENANT ERGENBRIGHT: What did you say?

JIM: Ben hurt a female student. On campus.

PRESIDENT WESSON: He hurt a female student?

JIM: He told me he had.

PRESIDENT WESSON: Why? When?

JIM: When did he tell me or when did it happen?

PRESIDENT WESSON: When did it happen?

JIM: Two days ago. When he was out at night walking.

PRESIDENT WESSON: Two days ago?

LIEUTENANT ERGENBRIGHT: *(To* JIM*)* What are you talking about?

JIM: I only want to make sure we all know who Ben is.

LIEUTENANT ERGENBRIGHT: Ben has not been walking around campus at night.

JIM: Yes, he has.

LIEUTENANT ERGENBRIGHT: Ben has not hurt anyone.

JIM: He told me he had. He said he was out walking and he saw a woman near the edge of the river. He said it was dark and he hurt the woman then shoved her into the water and ran away.

PRESIDENT WESSON: Why did he do that?

JIM: He was angry.

PRESIDENT WESSON: Who was this woman?

JIM: He didn't know.

LIEUTENANT ERGENBRIGHT: This didn't happen.

PRESIDENT WESSON: I don't believe anything like that's been reported.

JIM: I'm only aware of what I was told.

LIEUTENANT ERGENBRIGHT: Ben's not capable of something like this.

JIM: Ben isn't an innocent.

LIEUTENANT ERGENBRIGHT: I never said he was.

JIM: You implied he was.

LIEUTENANT ERGENBRIGHT: He's not capable of what you're describing.

JIM: Obviously you're wrong.

PRESIDENT WESSON: *(To* LIEUTENANT ERGENBRIGHT*)* He didn't mention any of this to you?

LIEUTENANT ERGENBRIGHT: I can't discuss what he mentioned.

PRESIDENT WESSON: He hadn't told you he'd been roaming the campus at night?

LIEUTENANT ERGENBRIGHT: I've told you I can't talk about any of what Ben and I have discussed.

PRESIDENT WESSON: He gave you no hint regarding this matter?

LIEUTENANT ERGENBRIGHT: He hasn't been roaming the campus!

PRESIDENT WESSON: So you don't know anything about the incident?

LIEUTENANT ERGENBRIGHT: I won't discuss anything with either of you.

PRESIDENT WESSON: Unless it serves to benefit you.

LIEUTENANT ERGENBRIGHT: That's not true.

PRESIDENT WESSON: You told me he felt he, "made a mistake". Is this another one of his "mistakes"? *(Pause)* During your conversations, did he confirm that he'd shot an Iraqi policeman's gun?

(A pause)

LIEUTENANT ERGENBRIGHT: He confirmed that, yes.

PRESIDENT WESSON: Did you have to ask him about it or did he tell you voluntarily?

LIEUTENANT ERGENBRIGHT: I asked.

PRESIDENT WESSON: He didn't mention it until you'd asked?

LIEUTENANT ERGENBRIGHT: No.

PRESIDENT WESSON: Did he tell you he'd told his classmates about shooting the gun?

LIEUTENANT ERGENBRIGHT: Yes.

PRESIDENT WESSON: Did he tell you about the dead and wounded men he'd seen?

LIEUTENANT ERGENBRIGHT: Yes.

PRESIDENT WESSON: Did he tell you about his dreams regarding a grotesquely slaughtered man?

LIEUTENANT ERGENBRIGHT: Yes.

PRESIDENT WESSON: Did he mention other times when he'd shot a gun?

LIEUTENANT ERGENBRIGHT: Yes.

PRESIDENT WESSON: Did he tell you he was wandering around campus at night?

LIEUTENANT ERGENBRIGHT: No.

PRESIDENT WESSON: Did he mention recently pushing or shoving a woman into the river?

LIEUTENANT ERGENBRIGHT: No. *(Pause)* Wait. Have you read that story which was given to Ben, *Man's Tooth,* by Steven Starley?

PRESIDENT WESSON: I have.

LIEUTENANT ERGENBRIGHT: Do you remember at the end of the story the main character grabs his girlfriend and shoves her into a river?

PRESIDENT WESSON: Yes.

LIEUTENANT ERGENBRIGHT: Mr. McFehren, is that right?

JIM: I'm not sure.

LIEUTENANT ERGENBRIGHT: That's what happens in the story, isn't it?

PRESIDENT WESSON: It is what happens.

JIM: It's not the same thing.

LIEUTENANT ERGENBRIGHT: It's similar.

JIM: Similar but not the same.

LIEUTENANT ERGENBRIGHT: So either Jim is lying about Ben's story—

JIM: —I'm not lying—

LIEUTENANT ERGENBRIGHT: —or Ben used the end of that story, telling Jim something he thought Jim wanted to hear.

JIM: I didn't want to hear that. And I'm not lying.

LIEUTENANT ERGENBRIGHT: Then Ben's just creating fiction. Again.

PRESIDENT WESSON: Violent fiction.

JIM: That's my point.

PRESIDENT WESSON: This sounds like recurring psychotic behavior.

LIEUTENANT ERGENBRIGHT: It's not.

PRESIDENT WESSON: So he's either a liar or a criminal.

LIEUTENANT ERGENBRIGHT: He's neither.

PRESIDENT WESSON: If an article were to show up in our campus newspaper stating that, along with what's already taken place, that Ben Navarro had now hurt a woman—

LIEUTENANT ERGENBRIGHT: President Wesson—

PRESIDENT WESSON: —or raped a woman—

LIEUTENANT ERGENBRIGHT: —rape?

PRESIDENT WESSON: — or lied to a professor about raping a woman—

LIEUTENANT ERGENBRIGHT: —President Wesson—

PRESIDENT WESSON: —and it was said the rapist had just returned from the war—

LIEUTENANT ERGENBRIGHT: —stop it—

PRESIDENT WESSON: —and if within that article there was a mention of an army psychologist's own ineptitude in helping the rapist—

LIEUTENANT ERGENBRIGHT: —enough —!

PRESIDENT WESSON: —we'd then be completely *dead to rights*!

(A pause)

LIEUTENANT ERGENBRIGHT: I need to speak with Ben.

PRESIDENT WESSON: Speaking with him won't change anything. There's no point to you or to any of us speaking with him. We'll get no honest answers. He's afraid to face himself. He lies to protect what he's done. Or what he hasn't done. He lies to protect the terrible situation he's created, making it all worse with every step.

LIEUTENANT ERGENBRIGHT: I need to speak with him again.

PRESIDENT WESSON: He covers himself up and with every step nears the ledge.

LIEUTENANT ERGENBRIGHT: I'm extending my stay.

PRESIDENT WESSON: He may have done what I'd feared.

LIEUTENANT ERGENBRIGHT: He hasn't.

PRESIDENT WESSON: You can't confirm that.

LIEUTENANT ERGENBRIGHT: Neither can you.

PRESIDENT WESSON: I can look into it.

LIEUTENANT ERGENBRIGHT: So can I.

PRESIDENT WESSON: Please do.

LIEUTENANT ERGENBRIGHT: He's done nothing wrong.

PRESIDENT WESSON: I hope you're right.

LIEUTENANT ERGENBRIGHT: *(To* JIM*)* I want you to stop speaking with him.

JIM: He's the one who called *me*.

LIEUTENANT ERGENBRIGHT: I don't care.

JIM: He's troubled.

LIEUTENANT ERGENBRIGHT: He's reactive.

JIM: It's true.

LIEUTENANT ERGENBRIGHT: He's stressed.

PRESIDENT WESSON: You've said that.

LIEUTENANT ERGENBRIGHT: He's only coping as best he can.

PRESIDENT WESSON: He copes inappropriately.

LIEUTENANT ERGENBRIGHT: He's confused.

PRESIDENT WESSON: You've already said that, too.

JIM: He's following his impulses.

LIEUTENANT ERGENBRIGHT: I'm going to speak with him.

JIM: He needs to honestly learn about the world.

LIEUTENANT ERGENBRIGHT: What does he need to learn?

JIM: That actions have consequences.

LIEUTENANT ERGENBRIGHT: He's aware that actions have consequences—

PRESIDENT WESSON: That terror and fear do not share space with rational civilization, that striking out only cultivates misery, that one's own irrational behavior rings and spreads like cracks in a pane of cut glass.

LIEUTENANT ERGENBRIGHT: Ben's behavior—

PRESIDENT WESSON: —is the burden he carries, the weight which holds him fast to the mud that surrounds and buries him.

LIEUTENANT ERGENBRIGHT: If he is sinking—

PRESIDENT WESSON: Mud is slippery, Mindy, it's a tricky place to set one's footing.

LIEUTENANT ERGENBRIGHT: *(To* JIM*)* Do you want children to die?

(A beat)

JIM: Do I want what?

LIEUTENANT ERGENBRIGHT: Do you want children to die in a sled accident?

JIM: Of course I don't.

LIEUTENANT ERGENBRIGHT: *(To* PRESIDENT WESSON*)* Do you want little children putting hard rubber balls into old people's mouths so that they choke on them?

PRESIDENT WESSON: What?

LIEUTENANT ERGENBRIGHT: In school I had to do a presentation on fetal alcohol syndrome. I had to research slide after slide of deformed fetuses, ragged and torn fetuses. And I once when I was twelve I found a small dog's head lying on the ground, beaten and bloody, it had been scooped out and emptied like a shell. I kicked it down the street into a neighbor's yard. *(Beat)* And one night when I was nineteen my mother slapped me in the face. I had said something crude to her and she became very upset and raised her hand and slapped me in the face. A moment afterwards, I attacked her. I hit her in the head and in the body with my fists, I hit her again and again until she fell. She screamed at me to stop. I didn't. I hit her until her nose bled and my own arms stiffened. When it was over, she crawled into a corner of the room. Her face was swollen and red and she started to show bruises. She asked me to get her a towel to wipe the blood but I refused. I walked out of the room and I left her sitting in the corner all by herself. *(Beat)* Ben is a good person. He's just confused as most of us are, at certain points in our lives.

(A pause)

PRESIDENT WESSON: Will that story be in your official report?

(A beat)

LIEUTENANT ERGENBRIGHT: Of course not.

(A pause)

JIM: Ben was troubled and was expressing honestly when he wrote what he wrote.

PRESIDENT WESSON: Yes.

JIM: The Lieutenant is right. Ben is a good person.

PRESIDENT WESSON: That very well could be true.

JIM: He is, in my opinion, *good*.

PRESIDENT WESSON: Perhaps if the correct procedure had been followed, perhaps if they had sent someone from the V A, someone who had experienced similar combat circumstances, perhaps then Mister Navarro would not have kept secrets. Perhaps then he would be less confused. Perhaps then he would have been more comfortable here at Prahl.

LIEUTENANT ERGENBRIGHT: I'm going to speak with Ben.

PRESIDENT WESSON: I would rather you didn't.

LIEUTENANT ERGENBRIGHT: That's not up to you.

PRESIDENT WESSON: We've seen your true colors.

LIEUTENANT ERGENBRIGHT: Is that right?

PRESIDENT WESSON: Someone with your rationale should be kept far away from Ben.

LIEUTENANT ERGENBRIGHT: You can't stop me from speaking with him. *(She crosses to her suitcase.)*

PRESIDENT WESSON: What is the name of your commanding officer?

(A pause)

LIEUTENANT ERGENBRIGHT: My commanding officer?

PRESIDENT WESSON: Yes.

LIEUTENANT ERGENBRIGHT: My commanding officer's name is Captain Dearing.

PRESIDENT WESSON: Captain Dearing?

LIEUTENANT ERGENBRIGHT: Captain Peter Dearing.

(PRESIDENT WESSON writes the name down in a note pad on his desk. A pause)

PRESIDENT WESSON: Can Captain Dearing be reached at Fort Gillem?

LIEUTENANT ERGENBRIGHT: He can.

PRESIDENT WESSON: Does he have a fax number?

LIEUTENANT ERGENBRIGHT: Yes.

PRESIDENT WESSON: Do you have his fax number handy or should I call Fort Gillem?

LIEUTENANT ERGENBRIGHT: I have it.

(LIEUTENANT ERGENBRIGHT *reluctantly picks up her bag and begins to look through it.*)

PRESIDENT WESSON: Please. No need to search for it now. If I need the number, I can call you at Fort Gillem. Or better yet, if I call Captain Dearing, I can ask him directly. No need to search through your bag.

(LIEUTENANT ERGENBRIGHT *closes her bag and places it on her lap.*)

LIEUTENANT ERGENBRIGHT: Thank you.

PRESIDENT WESSON: Of course. You're welcome. *(Pause)* Thank you for coming, again, Lieutenant. I'm sorry that everything couldn't have been salvaged a bit better, but it does appear most of this is can be blamed on simple things, simple things look to have cut short Mister Navarro's time here with us at Prahl. His attitude, his personal character, his own ideas of "time well spent." It all looks to have derailed him substantially and made appropriate action necessary. *(Beat)* If you need to phone anyone before you leave you may use our outer-office phone. But you probably have a cell phone. If you want to use our phone, just push nine first for an outside line. You may talk to whomever. *(Pause)* The path leads in many directions, but its ending remains constant.

LIEUTENANT ERGENBRIGHT: I should go.

PRESIDENT WESSON: Oh yes, well, Mister McFehren? Maybe you should complete the other action for which you entered my office in the first place?

JIM: Pardon me?

PRESIDENT WESSON: Would you like to say goodbye to Lieutenant Ergenbright?

JIM: Oh. Yes. all right, well. (*To* LIEUTENANT ERGENBRIGHT) Goodbye.

LIEUTENANT ERGENBRIGHT: Goodbye.

(JIM *and* LIEUTENANT ERGENBRIGHT *shake hands.)*

JIM: Have a safe flight.

LIEUTENANT ERGENBRIGHT: Thank you.

JIM: Thanks for your help.

LIEUTENANT ERGENBRIGHT: Yes.

JIM: I'm sorry both of us couldn't have done more.

PRESIDENT WESSON: Mister Navarro is a bright young man. Obviously, with the story he's written, with something more carefully thought out, he could someday decide to become a professional writer, if he'd like.

JIM: He'd do fine at that, if he chooses.

PRESIDENT WESSON: If not professionally, then as a hobby.

JIM: Yes.

PRESIDENT WESSON: He enjoys solitude, right Lieutenant? Him being an introvert? He enjoys being by himself. Like most good writers. Not attending school will be good for him, it will be a good lesson, I believe. All of this will be a good lesson for each of us, also. Especially you, Mister McFehren.

JIM: In the future I will certainly read all assignments first before I pass them out to the full class.

PRESIDENT WESSON: Good.

JIM: It was a mistake, not doing that.

PRESIDENT WESSON: Lesson learned. *(To* LIEUTENANT ERGENBRIGHT*)* Lesson learned? *(Beat)* These problems will all soon be in our past—Mister Navarro's, mine, yours—they'll soon all be in our past.

LIEUTENANT ERGENBRIGHT: Where they can't hurt us.

PRESIDENT WESSON: If you say so, then I'll believe it to be true.

LIEUTENANT ERGENBRIGHT: Goodbye.

PRESIDENT WESSON: Goodbye, Lieutenant. It was nice meeting you. Have a safe journey, and push nine, again, to use the outer-office phone if you need to. Just ask Jean, she'll show you where to go, which phone you may use.

*(*LIEUTENANT ERGENBRIGHT *nods. She picks her satchel from the floor and tilts her suitcase on its wheels.* PRESIDENT WESSON *opens the door for her and she exits.)*

JIM: I should get going, too. Have a nice rest of the week, President Wesson.

PRESIDENT WESSON: You also.

JIM: And we'll speak soon?

PRESIDENT WESSON: We'll get down to tacks.

JIM: Good.

*(*JIM *crosses to the doorway.)*

PRESIDENT WESSON: We'll get down to brass tacks and get it all smoothed out. Things will get back on track.

JIM: Oh yes? Great. all right. B-bye.

PRESIDENT WESSON: Goodbye.

(JIM *exits, shutting the door behind him.*)

(PRESIDENT WESSON *sits in his chair. He shuffles some papers. He becomes still.*)

(*Lights fade to black.*)

END OF PLAY